shine YOUR light

Your Guide to
Creative Inspiration,
Inner Wisdom & Happiness

Doreen Marcial Poreba

Printed in the United States of America

First Printing, 2017

ISBN 978-0-9980587-0-2

Published by
Creative Caboose
A division of The PR Czar® Inc.
610 SE Krueger Parkway
Stuart FL 34996

www.doreenporeba.com
www.creativecaboose.com
www.prczar.com

For information on individual or quantity sales, visit the website, www.creativecaboose.com, and email your request or send a letter to the address referenced above.

Book cover and interior design by Farah Rizvi Doyle
www.FRDdesign.com

Table of Contents

How To Use This Book

The purpose of this book is to inspire and guide you to awaken your creative spirit! Throughout the process of reading, reflecting and taking action, you will uncover and discover insights that may encourage you to make changes or move in a certain direction to enrich your life. You may decide to read this book at your own pace but the intention is for you to read one page per week as you reflect upon the theme and its corresponding photo. Then, throughout the week, with the theme in mind, carry out the suggested affirmations and exercises. Some of the tasks will ask you to record your thoughts, so you might want to get a notebook, however plain or fancy, and use it solely for this "Shine Your Light" process. You also can develop your own meaning to the photos and formulate your own activities surrounding the theme. Be creative! It doesn't matter which week of the year you begin. The day of the week doesn't matter either. You can do the readings in chronological order or open the book randomly each week. You may find that the selected theme is perfect for you that week. In the weeks ahead, if you randomly select the same theme again, it could mean you need to spend even more time with that theme's message.

This process will help you to consciously craft your life while experiencing your creativity. Have fun!

Requirements | An open mind, a creative spirit, an imagination, a notebook, a pen or pencil and a commitment to YOU!

The Inspiration Behind This Book

From the time I was 10 years old, I thought of myself as a writer. At that time, I declared that I would write a book some day. My interest in photography started at an even younger age. At age 8, I got my first camera by sending in Sugar Daddy caramel lollipop wrappers as part of a special offer. That camera would be my first of many. It could only produce black and white pictures. My, how far we have progressed! Digital color photography is now the norm. This is a book that features both my photography and writing, which is based on my own creativity, personal insights, observations and experiences. Two of my creative passions are writing and photography, so I thought it made perfect sense to publish a book of both my words and images intended to help inspire you! By engaging with this book, I hope you also will uncover, recover and discover your creative calling as well!

Acknowledgments

I have been blessed to have so many supportive people in my life and I am grateful for all of them. I wish to specifically acknowledge:

- David Crandall, his front porch and the beautiful Vermont view and surrounding creatures, all of which supported me 100 percent through the writing of this book

- Women Supporting the Arts, whose belief in this book and initial grant helped me get started

- My parents, for modeling the importance of creativity through their interests in photography, music and art

- Patty Jensen, my dear friend and a professional editor, who volunteered to review and edit the first draft of this book

- My English teachers at Windham High School in Ohio, who taught me the basics of good writing and inspired me to take my writing beyond homework assignments

- Eric Maisel, my creativity coach and author, who helped inspire and motivate me toward the completion of this book

- Julia Cameron for expanding my creativity through her book, "The Artist's Way," and Nancy Julian, for introducing me to this creative process

- God ... for all that is

Bonuses

Thank you for your purchase! Be sure to take advantage of these bonuses by going to www.creativecaboose.com/bonus.

1) A downloadable guided meditation to inspire your creativity, complete with sounds of nature and Native American flute.

2) A PDF containing 10 tips for unlocking your creativity set against one of my photos, suitable for framing.

3) An invitation to participate in a private "Shine Your Light" Facebook group where you can exchange ideas and observations with others.

inner & outer
BEAUTY

Who do you wish to see and be when you look at yourself in the mirror? Do you see yourself in all your glory — your beauty inside and out? Or do you see your blemishes, a body that is too fat or too thin or other aspects that don't please you?

Concentrate on seeing yourself exactly how you wish to be — not just externally but internally as well. Each time you look in the mirror, tell yourself — out loud — at least one positive attribute about yourself. For example, "I love my smile and how it brings happiness to others." Or "I feel an inner strength that helps me overcome any challenge." Don't think too long or hard when doing this exercise.

This week, go with the first positive statement that comes to you when you look in the mirror. It's OK to admire yourself because when you do, you are admiring others as well because we are all connected!

Affirm: "I love myself just the way I am!"

clarity in the
CLOUDS

We've all had the experience of noticing clouds that appear to have some sort of shape such as an old man's face or an animal. In the left photo, I see an angel with its head at the top and wings spread out on each side with a trunk falling below the wings. What do you see? The clouds in the right photo made me think of a cross and God.

The left cloud formation immediately grabbed my attention because it tied into a song that I had just sung that evening at a spiritual gathering. I had not been able to share the song publicly since writing it seven years prior when my best friend, Sue, had died suddenly. On the evening that I sang the song — which expressed how much she inspired me — I walked outside, looked to the sky, and saw this beautiful image of an angel. To me, it was a sign from Sue that all is well in her new world and to trust that my life also was in perfect, divine order.

This week, make a conscious effort to see if you can spot any "signs" or messages in the clouds. Recognize how fleeting the form may be. Carry a small notebook or perhaps a small camera or even your mobile phone camera and record your observations. You never know what awaits you!

Affirm: "The right and perfect message awaits me as I look to the sky and see clarity in the clouds."

owning your
AUTHENTICITY

Do you ever wear a mask to "protect" your real identity? Sometimes we put on a different face or we don't let our real personality shine through. We may feel a certain aspect of ourselves will not be understood or accepted. Or we're afraid that by speaking our truth we may be criticized so we put on a "mask," just as it appears this raccoon is wearing.

This week, be aware of encounters you have with others and notice if you are being completely authentic in your interactions. If not, why not? What aspect of yourself are you protecting? What would happen if you fully exposed your bona fide self to the other person?

Focus on being "real" — totally transparent in all of your exchanges with others. Catch yourself holding back and shift immediately. Observe your feelings as they're happening and then again later when you're alone.

Affirm: "I express my true nature by being transparent and authentic with others."

good morning, SUNSHINE!

There was a time when I used to walk along the boardwalk every morning and capture sunrises with my camera. After seeing so many, I realized that no two are the same. One day while walking, I became so inspired by the natural beauty that I wrote a song in my head. As soon as I got to my car, I wrote down the lyrics on a napkin, the only material I had to write on. When I got home, I added the music. I called the song, "God Paints A Picture," because I began to see each morning's sunrise as an individual, divinely inspired painting.

This week, plan to get up and watch a sunrise. Pick one day — actually build it into your schedule as if it's an important appointment not to be missed. Figure out ahead of time where the ideal location may be to observe it. You may want to bring a camera or just record the experience in your mind's eye.

Notice the different colors or perhaps one color will dominate. Also, make other observations, such as how the light reflects its surroundings.

Affirm: "I allow the magnificence of nature to permeate my soul. I fully experience the stillness and peace within."

LOVING
relationships

I captured these butterflies with my camera in the Florida Everglades. They appear to be mating. Watching them as they stayed together brought a sense of peace and freedom to my soul. To me, they represented a couple flying through life, loving each other and simply getting along.

Why do so many relationships fail to take off? Or sometimes, they begin with a magical connection and continue to develop, only to lose their spark or disintegrate entirely.

This week, concentrate on your relationship with others. Whether it's your mate, your boss, your child, your mother or father, a sibling or a friend — it makes no difference. Carefully examine each one and note your part and what aspects you could improve. Do you get defensive when the other person shares something negative about you? Do you overreact? How often do you go on the attack? Do you listen with "open ears?" Are you loving and compassionate? Make a commitment to take at least one action to improve your relationships and see what a difference it makes.

Affirm: "I am grateful for the relationships in my life. I feel freedom and lightness as I demonstrate my love to others."

facing your
FEARS

What are your fears — however large or small, sensible or illogical? One of my fears has always been frogs! I don't know where this fear comes from. I have no memory of my brothers ever putting one down my shirt (just that thought makes me squeamish) or any other memory of that nature, but if one suddenly hops in my path without warning, I will either scream, jump or both.

Your fears may not revolve around a creature. Perhaps you are afraid to allow yourself to love deeply because a partner in the past has hurt you. Or maybe you have a fear around money and that you will not be able to pay your bills this month. A very common fear is public speaking.

This week, face your fears — whatever they are — head on! Work with those fears of which you are already aware and notice any new fears that may come up for you. Meditate on what you can do to work through them. Ask yourself, "How would my life be different if I didn't have this fear?" Would I feel a sense of relief? More love? More peace of mind?

Affirm: "I release all fears. I exercise my strength, faith and wisdom to work through them."

TRAVELING
to your heart's desire

I visited Sedona, Arizona one day — literally. It was part of a quick, five-day trip to Phoenix, including my two travel days, so one day was all that I could fit in. I was overwhelmed with the area's breathtaking landscape of red rocks, blue skies and positive vibrations. I must return someday! In the meantime, I appreciate the awesome beauty in this photo.

Where have you visited that you wish to return for an extended stay? This week, allow yourself to revisit that place in your mind's eye. If you have any photographs, get them out and surround yourself with them. Bring out any other mementos that will enhance your experience.

This week, think of what it would take to get there again. Would it require flying or is it within driving distance? How much time would you like to spend there? Would you like to go with a group of friends, your family, your significant other or by yourself? What would it cost? Think of all of the details, then take action to make it happen.

Affirm: "I deserve to return to (insert your place here.) I have the heartfelt intention, the mindset and the action plan to make this happen."

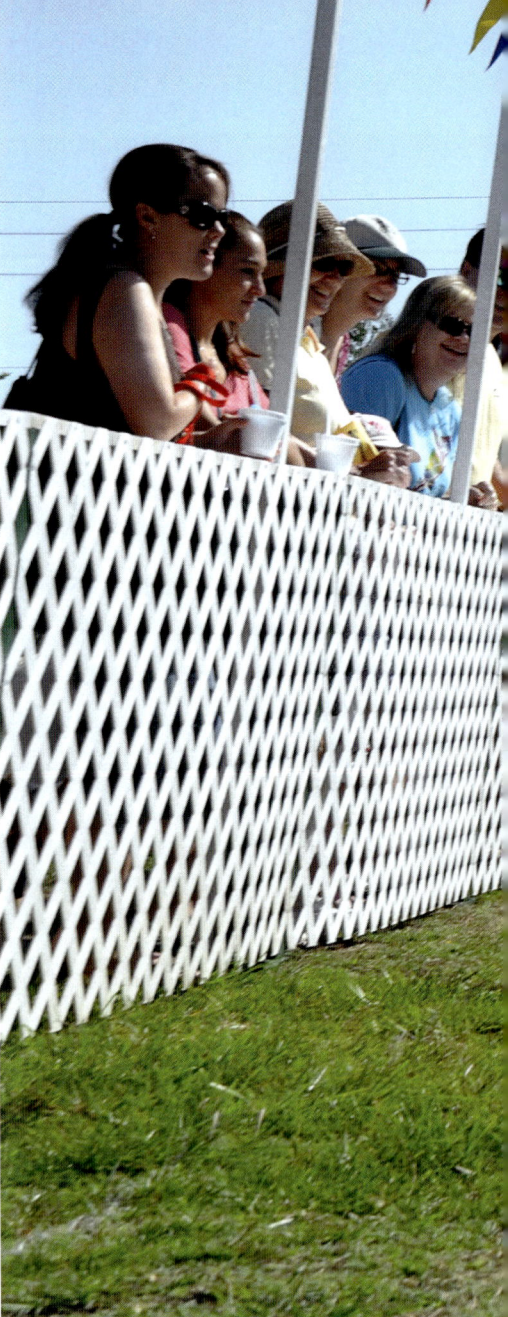

week 8

racing toward the
FINISH LINE

Do you find yourself frequently caught up racing toward a finish line? This destination could be the end of an important work project, shuttling your kids from one activity to another or just handling your day-to-day activities as if you're running a race. You may not even be able to see the end in sight!

This photo depicts the intensity in the dogs' faces as they're encouraged by their owners to race to the finish line. While there is nothing wrong with being intense while working toward your end goal, it's also important to have fun and not allow your stress levels to build in the process.

This week, as you're going toward whatever your finish line may represent, take time to close your eyes and take a few deep breaths. Think about other actions you can take that will allow you to enjoy the process itself and appreciate the steps along the way.

Affirm: "As I work toward completion, I take time to breathe and enjoy the process of moving toward the finish line."

anything's
POSSIBLE

If you've ever gone fishing, you know that when you cast your line into the water, you never know what you might catch. It could be a trout, a catfish, a dolphin or a shark, depending on the type of water. You could even hook an old shoe! Or you could spend an entire day coming up empty handed.

This week, when you cast your line into the sea of possibilities, you can improve your chances of "hooking" what you desire by taking time to center yourself each morning. Start by taking a few deep breaths while focusing on becoming present. Then set your intentions for the day and visualize what you wish to manifest. Do this before getting out of bed. Complete this exercise every day this week and check in at the end of seven days to see how you did! Feel free to add your own steps to the process that may work for you.

Affirm: "I am centered and present. I set my intention on (choose your goal) and I am visualizing it happening."

there is no
THERE

When I first viewed this landscape in Plymouth, Vermont, I was taken in by the gorgeous combination of the autumn leaves' colors. I also noticed the dirt road appeared as if it could go on forever with its winding pathway, so I decided to name it, "There is no There."

How many times have you told yourself — "When I get this job, then I'll be happy. Or when I have this amount of money, attract the right partner, get my new car, close on my dream house — once I get "there," I will be ecstatic!"

Have you ever noticed that when you get "there," there's always another "there"?

This week, focus on what's happening right in front of you. Allow yourself to be happy in the present moment. Notice how many times your thoughts drift into the future or you lament the past and return to the now!

Affirm: "I find happiness in the present moment and I enjoy the here and now."

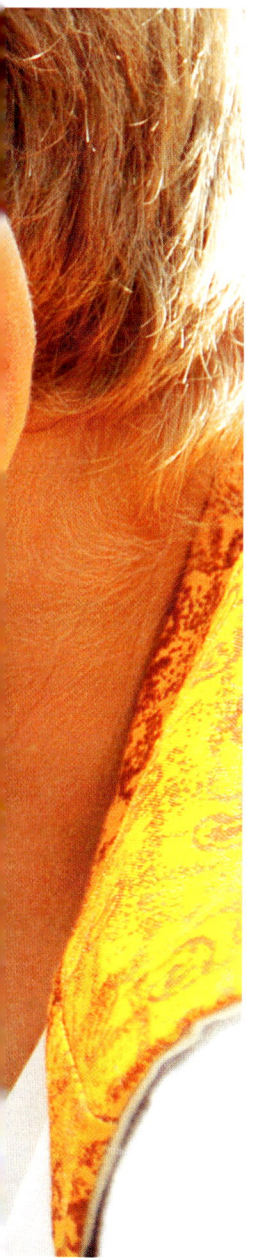

QUIET
contemplation

I took this picture of my younger son when he was nine years old. It's one of my favorite photos of him because I was able to capture him in what appears to be a true moment of contemplation. It's not easy catching an active young boy in this mode!

One of the definitions of contemplate is "to have in mind as a probable though not certain intention" and "to look thoughtfully for a long time."

Identify a special place that is conducive for meditating. If you live near water, it could be the ocean, a river or a lake. Perhaps a nearby woods or a favorite park calls to you. Wherever it is, go there, sit in silence and clear your mind for however long it takes.

This week, reflect upon what is really important to you. Afterward, ask yourself if your use of time and your day-to-day actions align with your priorities. If not, explore ideas on how to close this gap. We might say our family is most valuable but then we realize how little time we actually spend together.

Affirm: "As I reflect on what's really important in my life, I am filled with gratitude."

time for
TRANSFORMATION

For some reason, I've always been attracted to dragonflies and every now and then, one will come into my space and hover nearby. This particular dragonfly must have gone to modeling school because it seemed to pose, as if on command, as I photographed it from different angles.

I've read that dragonflies represent transformation. With that meaning in mind, when a dragonfly flies near you, it could be symbolic of a change that is needed in your life.

This week, take time to review your priorities and see if any changes are in order. They don't necessarily have to be big changes. Perhaps you've been staying up too late and need to go to bed earlier. Or you might benefit from a change in perspective about a particular subject. It's so easy to get stuck on one point of view. Be open to unanticipated changes as well.

Affirm: "I readily and openly create changes in my life that lead to a positive transformation."

pollinating
PLEASURE

Bees are quite productive creatures. You may have witnessed a bee pollinating a flower, which gives life to it, leading it to blossom. Some bees also spend time making honey. They can get your attention by stinging you. But rather than focus on discomfort, concentrate on the positive aspects.

What can you do to "pollinate" or "nourish" the life of another person, animal and yourself?

This week, focus on being joyful and sharing your bliss. Think of all the ways you can help someone blossom, however small. It could be as simple as smiling at a person who appears to be down. You never know how your actions might affect another's life. Or "pay it forward" by paying for the person behind you in a drive-through line at your favorite eatery. Relish in the feeling of knowing that you may have just made someone's day!

Affirm: "Through my words and deeds, I bring beauty into the world by helping others blossom."

Shedding
OLD STUFF

This butterfly didn't start off as a beautiful being capable of spreading its wings and flying. There was a time that it didn't have wings. It had to go through the various stages of being an egg, developing into a caterpillar, spinning a cocoon and then becoming a butterfly. Is your life in need of a metamorphosis? What stages are you going through now? Be very conscious as you move from one stage to the next because how you handle your own "chrysalis" will affect the outcome.

This week, examine whether it's time to shed any part of your life to make room for the next phase. Make a list of everything that comes to mind that you have been wanting to release but have been unable to let go. Include both emotional memories and physical "stuff" that you have thought about donating, recycling or trashing. Examine specifically why you are you hanging on. Oftentimes, the reason is fear. Fear of what? Identify the resistance for every item on your list. Then explore what would happen if you let go. Commit to taking one item on your list and setting it free!

Affirm: "I shed my old stuff to make room for the new. I spread my wings and fly!"

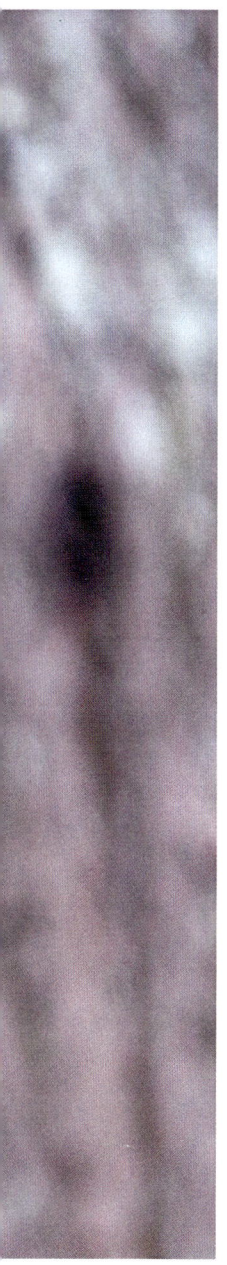

practicing
PATIENCE

Anyone who has ever tried to photograph a hummingbird in flight knows that it requires patience. These tiny birds usually don't hang around in the same spot for very long, even when there's a feeder around. So you wait patiently, and at just the right moment, press the shutter button to capture the action.

This week, practice being patient, especially when you most resist it. If you're in traffic and the person in front of you is going slowly, instead of getting annoyed and tailgating, take a deep breath and relax. Or you might find yourself in a situation with another person who is having a hard time seeing your point of view. Sometimes we grow impatient as we try to explain ourselves. We may find ourselves being constantly interrupted. Instead, recognize this as an opportunity to exercise patience.

At the end of the week, reflect on the instances where patience came into play. Reward yourself by going to your favorite restaurant. Take an extra long time to chew each bite as you savor the flavor!

Affirm: "I am patient as I appreciate each moment of my life."

expect the
UNEXPECTED!

How many times has something totally unexpected happened in your life? Sometimes these surprises stun you in a negative way and other times they elicit instant joy.

When I took this photo, my camera was set up on my tripod at a slow shutter speed as I prepared to capture the silkiness of a waterfall. All of a sudden, I heard a little girl's voice shout out, "Deer! Deer!" I swung my camera to the right and saw these deer peacefully coming out of the woods and into the water. It was a magical moment.

Although my camera settings were all wrong for this shot and I wished I would have had my zoom lens on my camera, I quickly adapted. Moments later, the deer vanished back into the woods.

This week, appreciate the unforeseen occurrences in your life. Because they are unexpected, you can't prepare. But you can consciously decide ahead of time that you will welcome and appreciate the unanticipated moments and know that you have the ability to make any necessary adjustments.

Affirm: "I appreciate and welcome unexpected events in my life and modify to receive optimal results."

EXPANDING
your opportunities

I gave myself the gift of attending a writer's workshop in Denver, Colorado. I had never been to this state so I was already excited but I decided to expand the opportunity even further by first visiting with my brother and his family, who live in Grand Junction, Colorado.

Then I got the idea to invite my mom, who lives outside of Dallas, Texas, to join me. As fate would have it, my flight itinerary had me change planes in Dallas en route to Grand Junction. My mom met me at the Dallas airport and off we flew to Colorado.

We spent the week sightseeing. The amazing natural scenes that we took in were simply breathtaking, as you can see in this photo that I captured outside of the Red Cliffs Lodge in Moab, Utah.

What opportunities can you expand upon in your life? They don't necessarily have to be "big" occasions or even involve money.

This week, focus on opportunities for growth, learning, connecting, traveling, loving or anything that comes your way. First identify the opportunity and then see how you might expand it even further. You can even look at past opportunities and consider whether there remains a chance to broaden them. Have fun!

Affirm: "I open myself to new opportunities and feel my life expand."

being in
FLOW

How freely does your life flow? Like this waterfall, do you feel your life is perpetually in flow? Although that's possible to attain, it's common for each of us to feel "stuck" from time to time, which prevents our lives from flowing.

This week, examine the various aspects of your life — personal and professional relationships, your emotional and physical health, your spirituality and any other areas you deem important. Is there any one part where you feel stuck or a lack of flow? Do you know why?

Pick one area that would benefit from a change. Then identify as specifically as possible the stagnancy and the reasons behind it. Take time to really explore this area. Write down what comes to you as

quickly as you can in your notebook. Carry it with you for the rest of the day and write down any additional thoughts that come to you. Sleep on it and write more in the morning and at different times during the rest of the week. Once you have exhausted all of the reasons, determine what steps you can take to create more flow. It could mean making minor adjustments or ridding that part of your life completely.

Affirm: "I am grateful my life flows freely like a waterfall."

Walking your
TRUE PATH

Each of us is on a personal journey. Every day we are free to make choices. Sometimes the choice is simple, such as deciding what to eat for breakfast. Other decisions have a far-reaching impact, such as choosing a career. Regardless of the nature of the choice, it's important to acknowledge we must walk our own true path and not the one other people persuade us to take.

Oftentimes well-meaning friends and family will try to guide us or influence us in a particular direction that feels counterintuitive to us. We may feel resistance. It's also possible that someone may push us in a direction that feels right and we align with his or her thoughts.

This week, pay attention to the decisions you make and assess whether they keep you true to your path. Do a symbolic exercise and literally find a path to walk. It could be a trail in the woods, a walk on the beach or even your own backyard as you walk the perimeter. As you walk, meditate about the choices you've been making and determine if they support your authentic path.

Affirm: "I trust my intuition as I walk my own path."

nurturing
NATURE

I'm not sure who was the first to say, "Take time to smell the flowers." It's a statement that has been repeated many times but seldom lived. We get so busy with our day-to-day lives, responsibilities and obligations that oftentimes the simple beauty of a flower or something else in nature gets taken for granted.

This week, make nature a priority. If you live in the country, this should be an easy task. City dwellers may have to work harder, but it's still possible to increase your awareness of nature's beauty. Weather permitting, get out in nature. Make it a point to look for things you never noticed before. You may have glanced at a tree in your backyard hundreds of times but maybe this time you detect that the bark has an unusual pattern. Write down your observations in your notebook. Then write a poem or creative prose about your experience and share it with someone you know who appreciates nature.

Affirm: "I appreciate the simple beauty of nature."

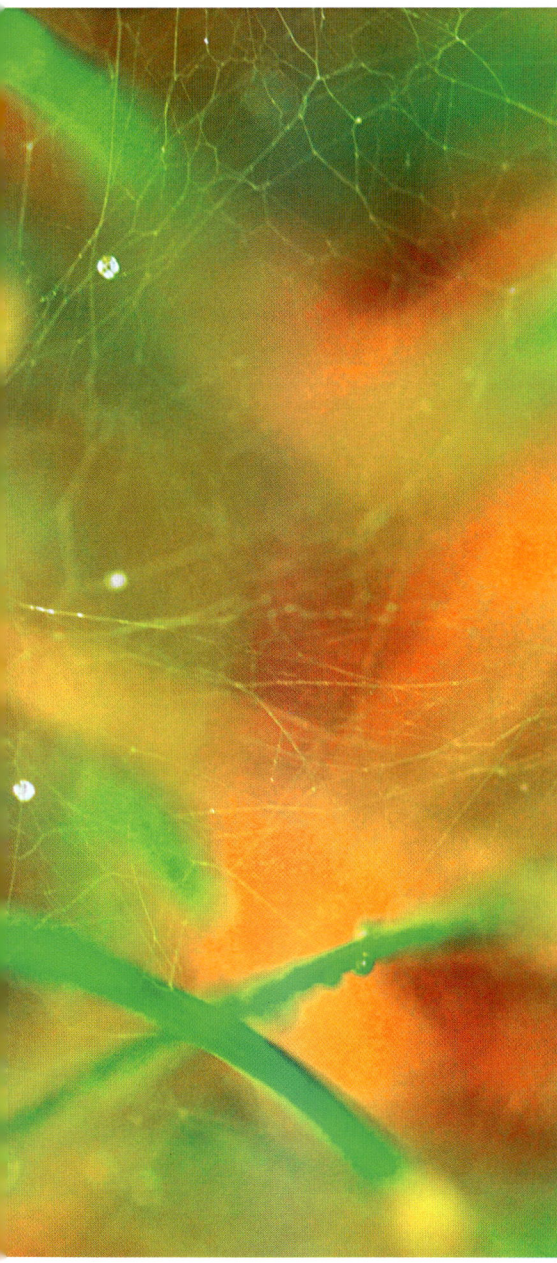

observing the
ORDINARY

How many times are we so focused on where we're going or what we want to accomplish that we miss the details along the way? Or we fail to see what's in front of us at all because we're so distracted?

This week, concentrate on slowing down so that you may observe the "ordinary" things in life and see them differently. Grass is something I walk on every day. On the morning that I shot this photo in Vermont, I leisurely and deliberately walked around the yard. I started to notice how pretty the dew droplets were on these blades of grass. Depending on the angle of my view, I could see sparkling, iridescent colors. I began to realize the symbolic connection of how we perceive issues in our lives. It all depends on our view.

Do you perceive your life situations to be dull and boring or vibrant and full of color? What details are you missing that might help you see things differently and bring about ease?

Affirm: "As I slow down and notice the details, I feel calm and relaxed."

one with the
UNIVERSE

I photographed this sunrise as part of an event called "Worldwide Photo Walk" in 2010 in downtown Stuart, Florida. It turns out this image was selected as the local winner of this worldwide competition. I believe part of the photo's attraction was the story the image told with the positioning of the camera. I've titled this photo: "Photographer: One with the Universe."

When I was shooting this sunrise, I felt a melding of myself with the natural beauty of the sun rising, the painted sky, the warmth upon my skin and knowing I was part of a worldwide photo event with people taking pictures in their locales at the same time.

This week, focus on your "oneness" with others and the universe. Pick one activity you can do to experience truly being part of the whole. Look online or in the newspaper for a group activity or invite friends and create your own mini-event. Here's where your creativity comes in!

Affirm: "I cherish the warm feeling of oneness with the universe."

CREATING
a new story

If I were to ask you to write a story based on this image, you could create a limitless number of scenarios. He's on vacation and taking a simple stroll on the beach. Or he just lost his wife and since then, walking the beach has become his morning ritual. We could invent as many stories as our minds would allow.

What is your story? When we look at our past, it's common to create a story about it and repeat it over and over — especially if the memory is a painful one. Sometimes we can get so stuck in our story that we can't move on.

This week, think about the "stories" you tell yourself and others. A bad childhood? Sticky divorce? Crazy boss? Psycho lover? Regardless of your story, know that you have the ability to change your viewpoint at any moment. Maybe that "jerk of an ex-husband or ex-wife" has been your greatest teacher because you learned patience, empathy and understanding and helped you get in touch with who you really are. Make a commitment to stop telling the same old story. Take one of your "stories" and change your viewpoint and description. Doing so may lead to a new, happy ending.

Affirm: "I am joyful as I add new story lines to my life."

playing with
PERSPECTIVE

We each see the world through our own filters. We can change how we view something depending on our perspective. In this photo of trees taken in Savannah, Georgia, I began playing with different angles and lenses. As I switched things around, I noticed different aspects and patterns. I realized how the possibilities were endless depending on my point of view.

This week, see what happens when you're engaged in a conversation with another person and you consciously change your perspective on whatever the discussion is about. Especially do this when you're not seeing eye to eye with another person's viewpoint.

Or practice changing your perspective as you think about a situation that's bothering you. Ask yourself, "What would happen if I thought about it this way?" Then write down your immediate reactions to the new thought in your notebook. Sometimes, all we need is a minor shift in our perspective to create a dramatic difference. Play with this concept this week and see if you notice any positive shifts.

Affirm: "Seeing the world through another lens brings new opportunities to me."

SILENCING
the crab in you

Have you ever felt like hiding out because you felt crabby? Perhaps this is a good week to seek some quiet comfort, even if you're not feeling irritable. What activities do you enjoy where silence and solitude go hand in hand? Maybe a bubble bath with candles and soft music playing in the background? Taking a walk first thing in the morning or late in the evening? The quickest way to combat crankiness or any feelings of negativity is appreciation.

This week, focus on everything for which you are grateful. Reflect on all areas of your life — from the everyday things you take for granted to the friends and family who nourish you. Make a list of everything and everybody you appreciate and notice how your mood shifts.

Throughout the week, each time you find yourself feeling the least bit uptight or stressed, immediately take note, silence yourself and focus on a state of gratitude. Notice how this shifts your state of being.

Affirm: "I appreciate the silence in my life, which creates an attitude of gratitude."

time to
PLAY

I wrote a song, "Time to Play," that became the title track to a debut CD that my music partner, Mike Jordan, and I recorded as the "Connected Souls" duo. The lyrics came to me at a time I was emerging from a challenging period in my life. One day, while hiking at a nearby park with a friend, an overwhelming feeling came over me that it was "Time to Play," if only I would get out of my way!

This week, make it a point to take on the youthful innocence of a child and get out there and play! Your activity could be as childlike as blowing bubbles or swinging on a swing at a playground. Use your imagination like you used to do as a child.

In fact, if you can recreate one of your favorite childhood pastimes, even better. Choose something fun that you haven't done in a long time. Invite your adult friends to play "Twister," or another game you enjoyed as a kid.

Be aware of the joy within you and see if you can schedule a fun activity into your life on a regular basis.

Affirm: "Getting in touch with my inner child allows me to feel playful."

RELEASING
your reptiles

In an audio presentation based on the book, "Entering the Castle" by author, medical intuitive and spiritual teacher Caroline Myss, she explains how St. Teresa of Avila refers to our reptiles as anything that qualifies as a struggle in our lives. Can you identify your "reptiles"?

This week, spend time identifying your primary reptiles. Do you struggle with addiction? Jealousy? Judging others? Gossip? Anger? Depression? Diet? Anxiety? Hone in on your top reptile and draw or paint a picture of the feeling behind this challenge. You don't have to consider yourself to be an artist to do this! Just play with the feelings that come up for you with either a crayon, pencil, pen, marker or a paintbrush in your hand. Feel the therapeutic benefits of releasing your feelings in this creative way. Then take some time to meditate on what came up for you and follow up by determining one action step to work on toward eliminating — or at least reducing — that struggle from your life. Choose a tactic that you haven't tried before or one that you haven't done in awhile.

Affirm: "I joyfully release the reptiles of my life."

childhood
MEMORIES

I took this photo while visiting my home state of Ohio near the house where I grew up. Seeing this old barn with the familiar ad quickly reminded me of my childhood and seeing this type of advertising.

This week, allow yourself to get nostalgic. Recall as many things from your childhood — games, images, people, favorite foods, best friends, sports, clubs, camping trips, vacations, teachers, stores and hobbies — anything from yesteryear that evokes a positive memory. Really tax your brain and see how many things you can remember and make a list in your notebook. Even if you had a difficult childhood, do your best to recall at least a few happy memories.

You'll probably find that you haven't thought about many of the items on your list in a long time. When you're finished, read your list out loud. You might even want to make a social event out of this exercise and invite friends over. Have them do the same thing and then share to see how many experiences you had in common. This should make for great conversation!

Affirm: "I appreciate all of my positive childhood memories. I smile as I reflect on each one of them."

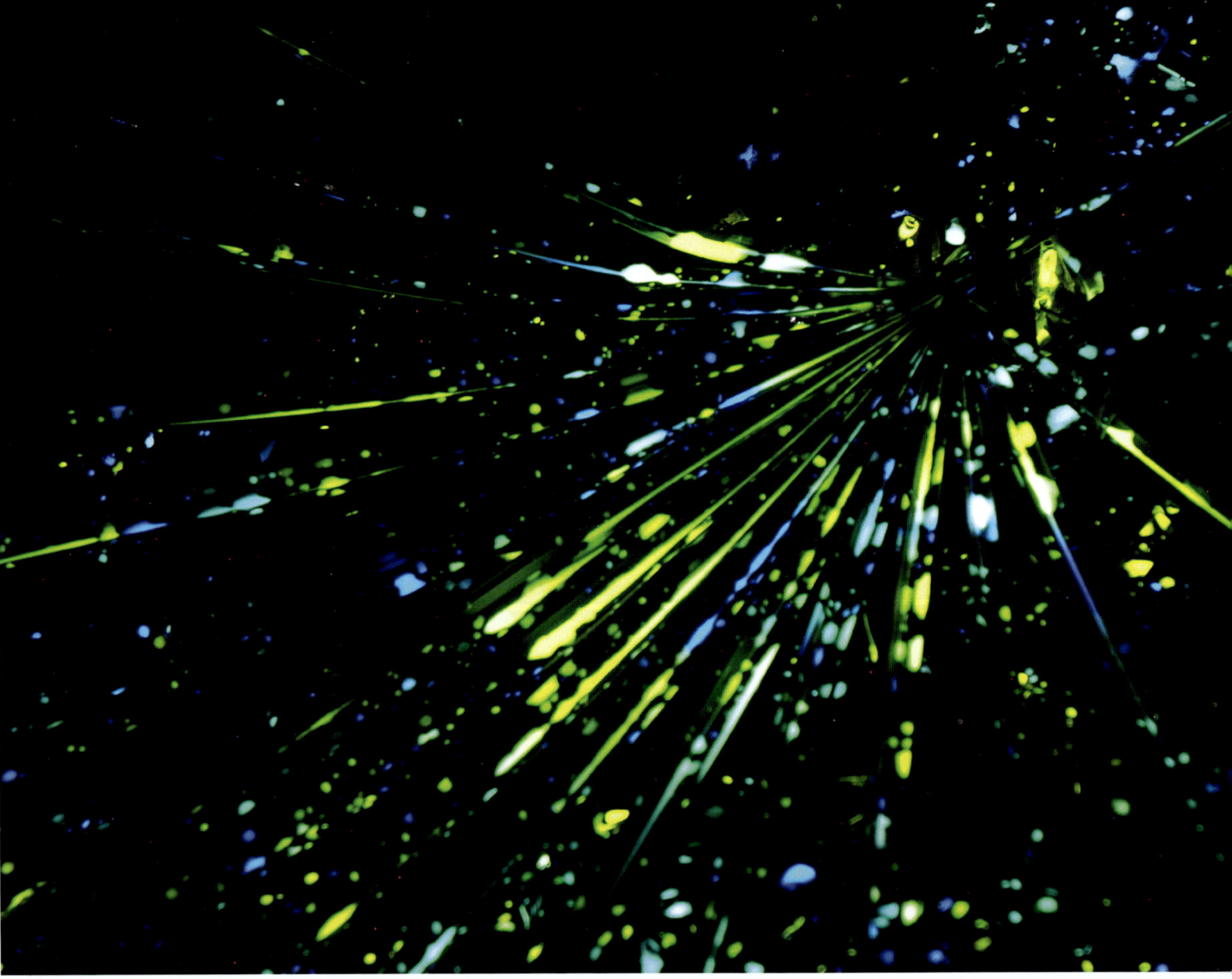

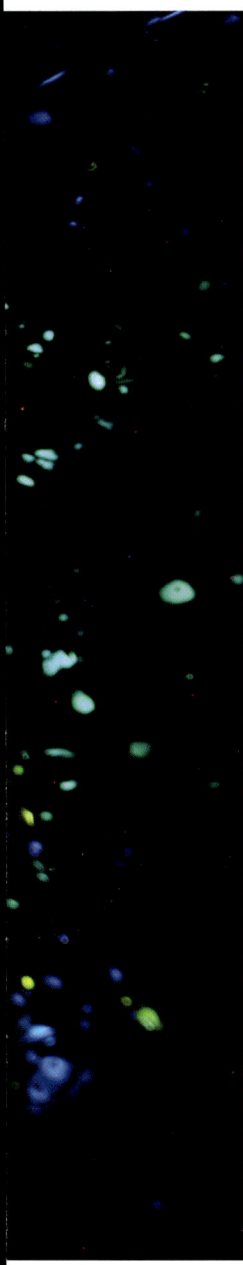

IMAGINATION
Station

I took this photo during a "Painting with Light" photography class. We shot "ordinary" items we found in the woods during our outing and used different colored gels to "paint" over them. When people view this photo, they're not always sure what it is. I respond by saying, "Use your Imagination." So often, we get stuck in ordinary thinking and we lose our creative spirit.

This week, focus on becoming an "Imagination Station." Allow yourself to get away from your everyday life and concentrate on imagining the life you want. When your "censor" starts to step in, silence it immediately!

At the end of the week, take out your notebook and quickly write down a list of what you imagined. Then take a sheet of paper, maybe even construction paper, and write a one-page essay titled, "The Best Day I Could Ever Imagine." Expand on what you wrote on your list. Decorate the page with stickers or add some artistic touches of your own and then post it in a place where you will see it every day.

Affirm: "I delight in imagining the best day ever!"

TRUST
is a must

This sunrise was one of the more unusual ones I've witnessed. I call it "Eerie Sunrise" because that morning there was a lot of fog and it felt "eerily" calm. Looking out at it gave me a feeling of "uncertainty" as to what the day held weather-wise and otherwise.

When you have moments of uncertainty, do you feel anxious or calm? Trusting or full of doubt?

This week, make a point of practicing faith and trust, particularly during situations that challenge you. Many of us believe in a "higher power" outside of us, within us, or both. Regardless of whether you call this power God, the Universe or Something Else, practice putting your faith and trust into the circumstance at hand, even if it feels "eerie." This practice could take the form of prayer, meditation or an artistic endeavor — anything that calms your mind and restores a sense of knowing that everything will work out as it should. Include whatever actions necessary to come to a place of peace.

Affirm: "Through my faith, I trust that all things happen for my highest good and I am at peace."

bringing
BALANCE
back

I captured this photo at a popular tourist spot in Savannah, Georgia. The live oaks and Spanish moss in all their splendor at Wormsloe Historic Site are the obvious attraction. They appear to create the perfect balance around the road. Sometimes our own lives may feel like a balancing act. Like a tightrope walker, if we lean too much one way we may sway or even fall altogether.

This week, examine whether you are keeping your life in balance. How well have you been juggling your personal, professional and spiritual desires? Whether you work inside or outside your home, do you consume yourself with work or projects so much that you neglect others — and yourself? Do you give the true priorities of your life enough attention? Make a list of your top five life priorities.

Then do an honest assessment of how you have been splitting your time among them. Once you are fully aware of your situation, make any necessary adjustments to bring your life back into balance. Notice any positive shifts in how you feel as you begin to align your priorities.

Affirm: "My life is in perfect balance as I focus on what is important to me."

refresh &
RENEW

Many of us have prayed for a miracle to happen at some point in our lives. To me — and I think just about every parent would agree — one of life's greatest miracles is the birth of a child. The whole process from conception to birth can be mind-boggling, especially if you've ever witnessed a baby's delivery. It can bring such an overwhelming feeling of joy that tears are often shed in that moment.

This week, look for one way to give birth to something. You don't need to think of this new activity as a miracle, but it should be an action you can take that refreshes and renews your life. Have you been thinking of taking a class or music lessons, trying a new recipe, learning to dance, exploring taekwondo or reading a book you bought months ago? Before the week ends, make a commitment to start one new activity that you believe will revive your spirit.

Affirm: "I reawaken my spirit as I give birth to (insert your action here) and feel the joy within me."

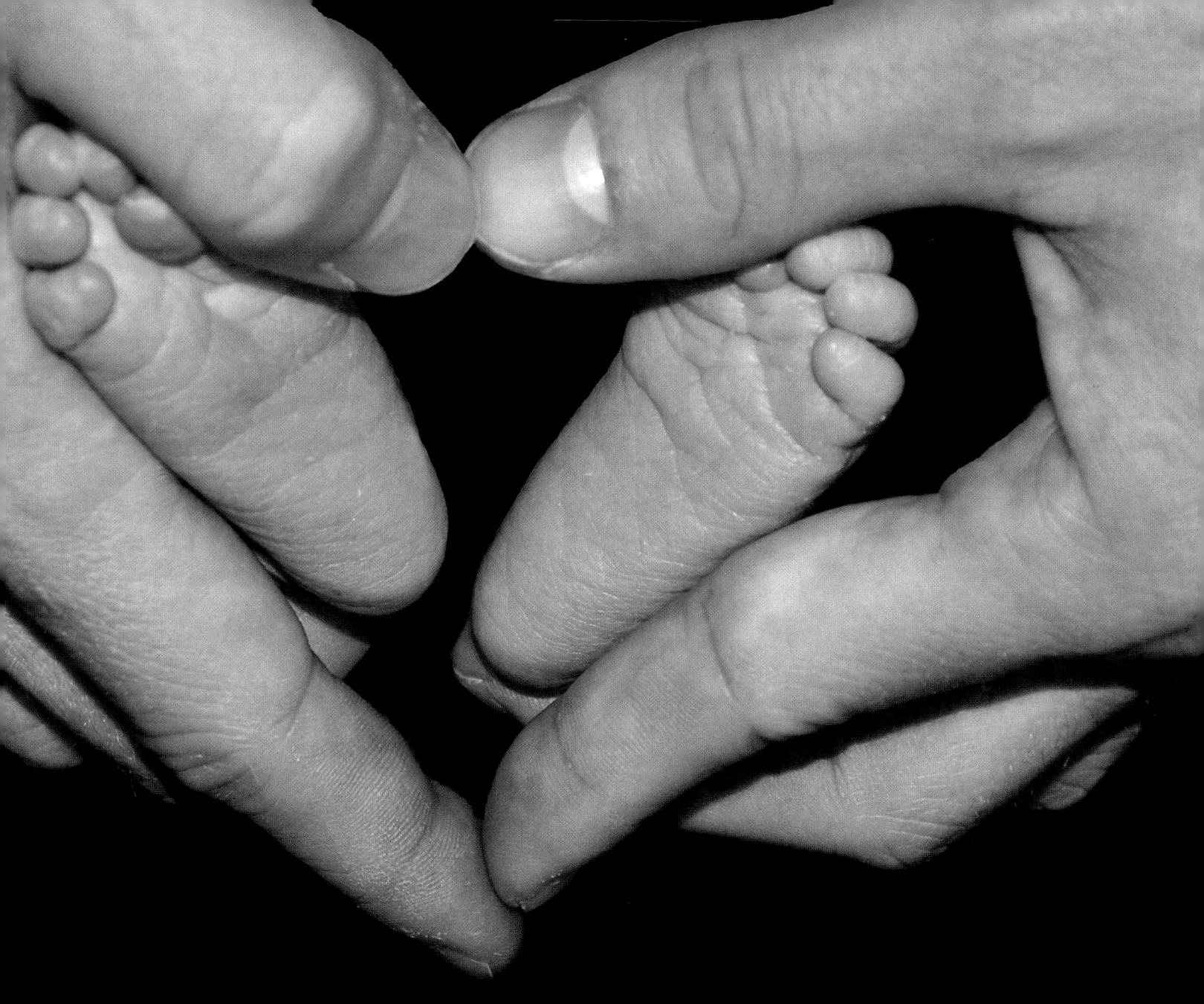

FREEDOM
in forgiveness

"Forgiveness sets the forgiver free." I first heard that statement while listening to an audio presentation by Dr. Joan Borysenko, who was referencing a *Time* magazine article on forgiveness. There are different schools of thought on this subject. Some people believe if there is no judgment, there is no need to forgive. In our humanness though, most people have had at least one experience, however big or small, where they have felt the desire or need to forgive.

Forgiving someone does not mean you condone the other person's actions and it is not about the "offender" — it's about you — because you are the one carrying around the "old baggage." It's hard to soar when you're carrying extra weight.

This week, examine your consciousness to see if you are still holding on to a past situation. Picture yourself carrying a heavy backpack that contains all of the negative emotion affiliated with it. When you get to the top, throw the bag over the cliff and feel the sense of relief — how much lighter you feel. Then imagine yourself as this bird, free to fly anywhere you wish!

Affirm: "I free myself to fly once again as I release judgment of (add person's name or situation here)."

gaining
CLARITY

This hawk appears to be intently focused. There are times we need to deliberately focus on an issue to reach a better understanding. The Quakers established "Clearness Committees" in the 1660s to help individuals gain clarity on personal or work issues with which they were struggling.

This week, call together four to six trustworthy people to serve on your Clearness Committee. Select a "focus person" to guide the committee. The committee's job is to provide a safe and supportive space for you to receive questions and respond however you choose.

You talk about your issue for 15 minutes and then, for the next hour, the committee asks open and honest questions about your issue to help you gain clarity. They do not attempt to fix the problem, provide therapy or carry out an agenda. The final 15 minutes are used to mirror back to you what they observed, without interpretation. The whole process is confidential.

If you don't have a particular issue to deal with this week, form the committee to help a friend in need and you can serve as the "focus person."

Affirm: "I gain clarity in a safe and supportive space."

go away, GOSSIP

Do you ever find yourself getting caught up in talking about others when everyone else is doing it, too? There's a name for that: Gossip. Resist the temptation to say anything negative about another person. If you're among a group of people and they start to gossip, you can choose to be quiet or "fly away" and find something more productive and meaningful to do. Better yet, make it a point not only to resist the gossip — also share positive comments about that person. Find at least one small attribute.

This week, make a fun game of it and come up with at least one compliment for every person you encounter this week. It can be as simple as telling someone how nice she looks today or how much you enjoy his laugh. Be sure to include those with whom you are not close and people who regularly challenge you.

Take it a step further and see what happens when you include strangers, such as someone who is in line at the grocery store. The only rule of the game is your compliment must be sincere.

Affirm: "I choose to see the goodness in others while leaving the gossip behind."

it's a SIGN

Whenever I see a breathtaking sunset, I am drawn to photograph the slowly changing scene. In this case, I didn't have my professional camera with me so I used my iPhone camera. When I saw the result, I immediately noticed how the reflection of the sun in the middle of the photo appeared to be a small image of a man. Perhaps he came into the picture to impart some kind of a message. Appearing to be full of light himself, maybe the symbolism was to always see the light in others and myself. How does this image speak to you?

This week, close your eyes each morning before getting out of bed. Think of a situation in which you need guidance and ask for some kind of a "sign." Then proceed throughout your days normally. Be aware that guidance or a sign may come to you when you least expect it. It could be a personalized license plate, a billboard, a song that plays on the radio, a commercial van that drives by with a saying on it or a penny you find with a date that has meaning.

Write any observations you make in your notebook. At the end of the week, check in with yourself to see if any signs led you toward a particular action or provided overall guidance.

Affirm: "I trust the perfect sign will be shown to me that will guide me in the right direction."

NO
regrets

On December 21, 2010, a lunar eclipse coincided with the winter solstice, an event so rare that this previous occurrence happened centuries ago in 1638. Even though I knew this event would not happen again in my lifetime, I was not feeling motivated to stay up to see it. But apparently, I was meant to witness this extraordinary sight, because I ended up not only waking up shortly after going to sleep, but then staying up and getting my camera to photograph the various stages. I'm so glad I did!

How many times have you missed out on something special, either because you failed to plan, found out too late or were too lazy or uninspired to take action for some other reason (or excuse)? One of the worst emotions to live with is regret.

This week, allow yourself to dream big and reflect on everything you've ever wanted to do, big or small. If you died today, what would you regret not doing in your life? Maybe it's not anything monumental. Perhaps it's speaking the words "I love you" to someone you hold dear but have never actually said those words to him or her. Whatever the case, identify those things you wish to do or say, then take steps to fulfill those desires.

Affirm: "I am blissful in living my hopes, dreams and desires."

NEW
beginnings

When I was just 24 years old, I was working as a television news reporter for the local ABC affiliate and was assigned to cover the first mission of the Space Shuttle Challenger. I decided to bring my still camera with me and after getting this shot, which later won an award, I was so happy that I did.

Although it was the launch of Space Shuttle Columbia that marked a new era in space flight, observing the Challenger, which followed Columbia, take flight was a first for me as I had never watched a space launch. Think of this week as a new beginning. Focus on starting or doing something new. Maybe it's something you've been putting off for a long time. It doesn't have to be too involved. It could be reading a book you purchased that has been sitting on your shelf or starting to write the book you've held in your mind for some time. Or trying a new recipe, taking an art class, planting a garden — anything that will energize you or bring a sense of satisfaction. Another option is to make your new beginning something internal. Look at a problem you've been having and view it in a new light.

Affirm: "I appreciate new beginnings in my life."

HELPING
hand

If you've ever observed squirrels roaming around in a park, they don't miss too many opportunities to nourish themselves. Offer them a peanut and they will eagerly take it out of your hand.

When someone extends a helping hand to you, do you find it difficult to accept his or her help? Or do you willingly and gratefully allow the person to help you? Sometimes when we could use some assistance, we resist asking for help and even if it's offered, we're too proud, independent or embarrassed to accept it.

This week, be proactive. Allow yourself to be nourished. Ask for help when you need it and gracefully accept it when it's offered.

I'm not the best cook and can sure use help in that area. Other times I could use another's feedback in solving a personal problem. If you don't feel you need help with anything this week, offer your assistance to another person. Consider your strengths and who might benefit from them, then be proactive and reach out.

Affirm: "I appreciate the people in my life and gracefully accept their help."

becoming
WHOLE
again

We are all made up of pieces that make us whole. Like a bird that loses its feather, sometimes we lose a part of ourselves. We may be oblivious to the loss or consciously let go of that which no longer serves us. We want to feel whole again. I was once in a relationship in which I became so confused that I slowly began to lose essential parts of myself. When that relationship ended, I realized I needed to "pick up the pieces" and rediscover who I really was meant to be.

This week, check in with yourself to see if you have recently left any "feathers" behind. Do you miss those parts of yourself or was it necessary to shed them? Losing a feather may or may not make a difference. Only you can assess what is OK or actually needed to discard. Also examine which aspects of yourself that you may need to "reattach" or rebuild. Through this process, you may even discover new aspects of your true self. It is important to do this process without a sense of self-judgment.

Affirm: "I love who I really am as I go through my process of self-discovery and become whole again."

puppy
LOVE

How could anyone not be drawn in by the innocent look of this puppy? The truth is, puppies can teach us about unconditional love. It doesn't seem to matter if we're having a bad day and are in a bad mood, they love us just the same. They give us their love with "no strings attached." How many of us can honestly say we love those in our lives with no conditions?

This week, examine your close relationships. What expectations do you have of others? How do your moods or reactions fluctuate when someone you love disappoints you? How quickly can you move past the other person's transgression and return to a state of love? Do you continue to hold a grudge?

The next time you're angry with someone you love, picture this person with the face of this precious puppy. Feel the unconditional love expressed in this pooch's face and work toward loving unconditionally.

Affirm: "As I let go of expectations, I practice loving others unconditionally."

finding
PEACE
within

Gazing at the sun setting is like watching a symphony orchestra perform its final piece of the evening. Both experiences signal an ending of something special that can leave you with a peaceful, pleasurable feeling within yourself. A sunset appeals to your visual sense while music heightens your hearing sense. Tuning into your various senses may help you attain inner peace on a regular basis.

This week, check in with yourself several times during the day and evening to see if you are able to experience a feeling of peace. Monitor yourself to see how long you can maintain this feeling, once achieved. Are you getting enough rest or are you pushing the limit? That alone can affect your level of peacefulness.

Make a list of activities in your notebook that you believe will produce peaceful feelings within you. Then practice some of them during the week. Your list may include watching the sun set or rise, listening to relaxing music or curling up with a good book.

Affirm: "I appreciate the peaceful feelings within me."

MOUNTAINS ARE HIGH,
valleys are low

As a young teen, one of the first quotes I related to was "Life is a mystery to be lived, not a problem to be solved." I liked it so much I bought a poster with this saying that I hung on my bedroom wall. Those words resonated with me more and more as I got older and realized that life's natural rhythms would lead me on a journey of experiencing highs and lows, as serenely depicted in this photo as hills and valleys. The key is in how I respond whenever I find myself deep within a valley. I have learned to appreciate the valleys as opportunities — to grow, to learn, and to climb to the next level.

This week, focus on seeing your valleys or low points as opportunities for growth, however, do not look too far ahead. Appreciate where you are in the present moment. Allow yourself to feel your feelings, accept them, and trust there's an opening waiting for you beyond the horizon. As soon as you catch yourself either looking backward at a negative situation in your past or worrying about the future, stop yourself immediately. Get back into what author Eckhart Tolle coined as "the now."

Affirm: "I appreciate the present moment and view any valleys of my life as opportunities for growth."

THRILL
of a lifetime

I've never been at the control panel of an airplane commanding death-defying displays but my guess is that being in such a position would be thrilling. When is the last time you piloted a true thrill in your life? Can you even name one experience that would electrify you?

This week, spend some time thinking about what would be thrilling, breathtaking, awe-inspiring or exhilarating for you to experience. Let go of limitations as you search your mind — and your heart. Have you ever thought about skydiving, driving a race car, mountain climbing or white water rafting? Or maybe you want to experience the world's scariest roller coaster. Perhaps a thrill to you doesn't involve the physical so much. You might find it exciting to meet someone famous.

You could plan to be in the audience of your favorite TV show.

Allow yourself to search beyond your typical boundaries of thinking. Make a list off the top of your head and write down your ideas as quickly as you can. Then choose one, do whatever research is necessary and begin taking steps to make it happen. You can do it!

Affirm: "I am energized as I take steps to make the thrill of my lifetime happen!"

creating &
INNOVATING

As a freelance photojournalist on assignment with a magazine, I was given the enviable opportunity to write about and drive the world's fastest street legal production car, the Bugatti Veyron 16.4 Super Sport. Its record speed was clocked at an amazing 268 mph and it sports a number of innovative features. This $2.85 million vehicle is a remarkable example of what can be created when limits are removed.

This car is so impressive, that as I drove on the highway, I noticed heads turning from every direction to catch a glimpse and everyone from kids to adults attempting to take a snapshot of it with their cell phones.

This week, focus on innovation, either in your professional life, personal life or both. It's not so much about "turning heads" as it is for you to feel a sense of freedom and release as you create anew.

When faced with an issue or asking yourself what you wish to do this weekend, be creative. Take a new approach to an old problem or plan something you've never done before, even if it makes you uncomfortable. Getting out of your comfort zone leads to growth and activities you may never thought were possible.

Affirm: I enjoy a sense of freedom as I allow myself to be creative and innovative."

seeing
SUNSHINE
through the rain

Every summer, I drive by this brook daily. One day I was moved to photograph it because I noticed that it appeared to be much fuller than usual after two days of continuous rain. The rushing sound of the water caught my ear while the smoothness of the flow grabbed my eye's attention.

When rain seems to be pouring down on your life and there's no sun to be found, are you able to see the benefit? You may not be able to appreciate the result right away, but hopefully you can eventually.

This week, take time to reflect on those times when you couldn't "see the light." Draw upon past experiences or look at what's going on today. Quickly make a list of experiences that come to mind. Then list the "up" side to each one. For example: I lost my job. Benefit: I was forced to look for a job that suited me better and I found a higher paying, more satisfying position.

We all have the potential to flow as freely and peacefully as this brook if we allow our lives to rise and fall naturally.

Affirm: "My life is in perfect flow and I am at peace."

flying
SOLO

Some people fear being alone worse than death itself. Other people love spending so much time by themselves that their greatest challenge is doing activities with other people. Being alone becomes a habit for them.

This week, whether you spend a lot of time alone or hardly any by yourself, find an activity that you've never done on your own. Like this cedar waxwing bird, pick your own tree and branch out! Put on your creative thinking cap and brainstorm different ideas. Have you ever gone to the movies by yourself? Dined alone?

You might pick a restaurant with a cuisine you've never tried or plan a day trip to a place you've never been. Whatever you choose, while you are alone, tune into your feelings and record your observations. Do not censor what comes to you. Just write it down as quickly as it comes to you. This kind of reflection should ultimately bring you clarity. Focus on truly being present and savor each splendid moment!

Affirm: "Flying solo rejuvenates my soul."

'til death do us PART

Meet my "girls," Bebot and Angel, probably the most photographed dogs in the world! Bebot came to me as a total gift from the universe from someone I met in a small café while having lunch. I also consider Angel to be a tremendous gift. I initially fostered her from the Humane Society of the Treasure Coast and then adopted her. Upon receiving both of them, I made a commitment — 'Til death do us part."

This week, examine the commitments you have made. Have you kept them? Why or why not? Have you made a pledge or promise to another person, a group of people, yourself, a higher power, a charity, your job or animals? If you choose not to honor a commitment, it's important to understand the reason, especially if it has become a pattern. Sometimes we break pledges because we said "yes" when we meant "no" at the time we were asked to get involved.

If you have been thinking about taking an action that requires ongoing dedication, revisit it. If it's something that still interests you, make your vow and stick with it! Otherwise, honor yourself by only committing to what truly resonates with you.

Affirm: "I honor my commitments to myself and others."

the magic of
FRIENDSHIP

I feel blessed to have so many loving, caring friends. Sometimes we talk about getting together and it doesn't happen. When it does, I really appreciate the opportunity for connection. When was the last time you planned an outing with friends, one that was bonding and meaningful?

This week, take a leadership role in planning some type of gathering with your closest friends that will bring joy to all of you. It doesn't have to be expensive. You might invite them to your place for coffee, tea and dessert and just talk and play a game. Or let your imagination soar and plan a group activity you've never done before.

Your only goal is to enjoy each other's company — to connect with one another, smile a lot and laugh even more! Think of the last time you laughed so hard you cried and what it took to make that happen.

Affirm: "I am grateful for my friends and the love and caring that we share."

slow &
STEADY

Proceeding through life at a "snail's pace" isn't always possible or even recommended for certain tasks and activities yet slowing down and staying present can yield great benefits, such as appreciating precious moments that might otherwise be missed. Going at a nonstop pace day to day often causes us to make mistakes and can result in additional stress.

Do you find yourself often rushing through your morning routine? Are you racing through your day so quickly that you miss opportunities? This week, reflect on how fast you are moving through your life. Sometimes the slightest happening that slows us down can be annoying, such as following someone in a car who is going under the speed limit or getting every red light while driving. Instead of getting frustrated, take such occurrences as reminders to slow down and enjoy the moment.

Affirm: "Slowing my life to a snail's pace allows me to appreciate the moments of my life."

releasing
JUDGMENT

While hiking through the woods near Asheville, North Carolina, I came upon this fallen tree. I immediately noticed that it had the appearance of some type of creature with a distinguishable, long snout — kind of like an alligator. You may see an entirely different image when looking at it, like when you look at cloud formations. The same applies when we meet someone for the first time and even subsequent encounters. Initially, we tend to draw conclusions on looks alone.

This week, notice how quick you are to judge when looking at a person for the first time. It could be a customer with multi-colored spiked hair in line at a grocery store, a woman wearing excessive jewelry at a business meeting or a tattooed teenager who pulls up next to you in a car with music blaring. How many times have your first impressions been inaccurate?

As you look at different people this week, notice your initial reaction and then focus on releasing judgment. Observe whether it makes a difference in how you feel. Do you feel lighter? More compassionate?

Affirm: "I release all judgment of others and accept them as they are."

soaring to new
HEIGHTS

Each of us has the potential to live a more colorful life but we all could use a little pumping up from time to time. Like this deflated hot air balloon, we can see the brilliance of its colors but without the hot air to inflate it, it remains lifeless and grounded.

This week, seek out friends, family or activities that will help you soar to new heights. Sometimes what we need are encouraging words spoken by a friend. If that's the case, reach out to your friend and let him or her know that you need to be uplifted. Together, plan an outing that will inspire both of you. Or engage in an art activity, take a quiet walk in the park, listen to your favorite music with headphones on or reward yourself with an exhilarating new experience, such as riding in a hot air balloon. You know yourself best, so take the initiative and choose what you know will work for you.

Affirm: "I choose to engage in activities that add color to my life and help me reach new heights!"

About The Author

Doreen Marcial Poreba, APR, (www.doreenporeba.com) has a love for "all things creative." In addition to writing this book, she also authored the book, "Idiot's Guide: Unlocking Your Creativity," which was published by Alpha Books, A Penguin Random House Company. She also offers an eight-week course, "Unlock Your Creativity with Spirituality," on bit.ly/porebadailyom, and is an award-winning photographer, singer-songwriter-musician and recording artist who released a CD of original music titled "Time To Play."

An accredited PR professional, she founded The PR Czar® Inc. (www.prczar.com), a full-service public relations firm in Stuart, Florida, in 1997. In 2010, she added a creative division called Creative Caboose (www.creativecaboose.com) to conduct creativity workshops for businesses, nonprofit organizations and associations. She also works one on one and with groups to help them recognize and fulfill their own creative potential. She earned her certification as a creativity coach from The Creativity Coaching Association. A magna cum laude graduate of Slippery Rock University in Pennsylvania, she has won more than 60 professional, public relations and photography awards during her career.

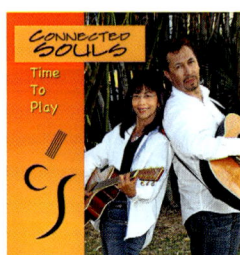

DailyOM

Be sure to take advantage of your bonuses at **www.creativecaboose.com/bonus.**